SOMETHIN' OUT OF NOTHIN'

Written by Sharon Shrum
Illustrated by Sandy Woodward

In elementary school, I didn't know I was different. I didn't know I was poor. I didn't know that some adults felt sorry for me because of what I looked like and where they believed I came from.

I didn't know that some adults believed that they were better because your family didn't have much money. Then, I went to middle school and that all changed.

I was really small for my age. My hair was thin and kind of stringy, not like other girls. They had thick, clean, brushed hair with bows or barrettes that matched their outfits. I was lucky to find a hair brush in the morning.

My clothes were clean, well most of the time. We shared clothes, even if they were my brother's clothes. We got one pair of shoes a year, and they were usually used, but they were new to us. We never had a coat until late in the winter for some reason. Most of my clothes came from a yard sale or passed down from my cousins. It was hard for my parents to clothe eight kids of their own plus two more kids who were my cousins that lived with us.

One of the best things about my childhood was school. I went to school every day. The warm bus would come and pick us up and I got to sit wherever I wanted. It wasn't like riding on the back of a pickup truck in the winter to go places, even though that didn't happen too often.

I hated to miss school. It was neat and clean and organized. It was warm in the winter and cool in the summer, and I always got to eat lunch. I had to scrape the trays to pay for my lunch, but I didn't mind. Mom said we didn't take handouts and it was good to work for what you got. So my brother and I scraped trays to pay for our lunches. A couple of other poor kids did this on their lunch too. Scraping trays was a whole lot better than having to tell the lunch lady that you didn't have any money. Plus, I got to keep the fruit and milk that the other kids didn't want. I filled a large paper bag and took the leftovers home on the bus each day. No one said anything and my brothers and sisters loved it. I felt so grown up scraping trays. I am not sure the other kids knew I was earning my lunch, and if they did, they never said anything.

    The second thing I loved was my math teacher. I loved math class and my teacher loved me. She had big blondish-brown hair with lots of hairspray to hold her hair in place. It never moved when she would get so excited and she danced around the room when we got a problem right. She was so smart. She was very funny too. It was usually just me laughing when she said a joke or something funny and she would always look at me and smile. She was always so clean and dressed very nicely. She had painted nails that matched her outfit. She smelled really good, like soap. She hugged me everyday. She even told me one day I was going to be a math teacher and she even wrote it on my report card for my parents to see. Oh, how I loved her. Sometimes she would even ask me to watch the class while she went to the bathroom. She trusted me so much she sent me on errands around the school when she needed to get a message to one of the other teachers or needed a soda from the teacher's lounge.

One day Mrs. Days, my math teacher, told me to take a note to the social studies teacher, Mr. Zarow. He wasn't in his room so I just started going around the school looking for him. When I walked by the teachers lounge, a few teachers that I recognized were talking to Mr. Zarow. I overheard one teacher say, "those Dawson kids were not going to amount to nothin'." Dawson was my last name. I had five brothers and two sisters who were the Dawsons too. Our house was always noisy. It was like we had enough kids in our house that could fill a classroom. Anyways, as I was walking by the teacher's lounge I kept listening. I probably should not have done that but I always listened to everything, even when I wasn't supposed to.

I figured it was ok because I heard my name so I thought someone was talking to me, not about me. I listened a little longer and Mr. Zarow agreed with the other teacher about us not amountin' to nothin'. He even shared a story about us kids. He said, "yea, I know what you mean. Everytime I go down to the golf course, I pass them on that back road and they are out on the road, playing in a mud puddle and waving at the cars. It's like they have no sense. They never have shoes or coats on."

We always waved at people, so he was right about that. Mom said that was just being nice. We were always supposed to respect people and be nice. We knew him so we waved extra hard at him when he came by. I was not sure why that was a bad thing. He never waved back. He just stared.

I slowly interrupted the teachers and said excuse me, and I told him that Mrs. Days gave me a note for him. They both just looked at me and then I walked away. I wonder now if they think I overheard them talking about me and my family. If they did they never said anything.

I went home that evening on the bus and thought about being nothin' the whole way home. What was nothin'? Why were they talking about me and my family? I didn't understand. I thought people were supposed to love each other and take care of each other, especially teachers. I thought they were supposed to care about children like Mrs. Days did.

    I had to try and put it out of my mind. When I got home, everyone seemed upset in my house. I didn't know what was going on at first and then I heard my parents talking about money and supper. There was no money and I was not sure if we had anything for supper. The fridge was empty and it was getting late. The little kids were playing quietly and the big kids were talking and staying out of sight from my parents. My parents were just angry. We knew not to get in their way when they were angry. I remember that week being a hard week for my family. It was late January and it was almost my birthday. Birthdays didn't really mean too much in my house.

We never had money to celebrate them. No one got presents like you see on TV, no one got a cake unless there was cake in the house that came off of my grandfather's pickup truck bed where he used to get day-old bread, cakes, and pastries behind the grocery store to feed his hogs. His first stop was at our house to let us pick anything that we wanted before the hogs got it.

Yes, I mean hogs, pigs, better known as swine to smart people. We thought we had struck gold getting on that truck. Rye bread, wheat bread, white bread, honey buns, cakes, jelly rolls, donuts, cinnamon buns, and more! The smell was like going to heaven! We loved it when that truck pulled into the yard.

Anyways back to my story. As I said, it was a hard week for my family. My dad was out of work for a while and he had just gone back to work that week. It was good news that he started working again. He scraped the money together for gas to get to work every day that week and we could not wait for Friday. Friday was payday! We all looked forward to paydays. We would always go to the grocery store on payday. That week we had made it to Thursday. Meaning, we ate every day that week and there was enough food to go around for all of the kids and my dad. I know sometimes my mom wouldn't eat just to make sure all of the kids ate.

That evening my mom went into the kitchen and the only thing that was in the kitchen was a 10 pounds bag of potatoes. I don't think it was a full bag because the burlap bag was not full. My mom peeled the potatoes real thin. You could probably read a newspaper through the skins. She knew that was all she had and that was the last of the food until tomorrow when daddy got paid. She made fried potatoes. She picked up the 5 pounds can of lard and scraped enough grease from the can to fry the potatoes. She made fried apples out of the apples I brought home. She put salt and pepper on the potatoes and cinnamon on the apples. She sent my brother to the cellar for the last jar of canned tomatoes that she had put up last summer. She put some potatoes and a little bit of apples and tomatoes on a plate for all of us. My dad got more because he worked and he got the ones that were slightly brown because she knew he liked those.

I remember after dinner she looked as though she had a sigh of relief on her face. All of the kids were fed. That always made her happy. Then all the kids went in to take a bath one or two at a time. There were ten of us so it took a while. When I was waiting for my turn, I heard daddy say, "you could always make somethin' out of nothin'." She said, "I guess I got it from my mom."

When I heard "somethin' out of nothin' I thought to myself, so nothin' is somethin', so I must be ok because I am somethin' and those potatoes sure did taste like somethin'. I never told her or my dad about the comment the teachers made, and I never did tell them about school that day.

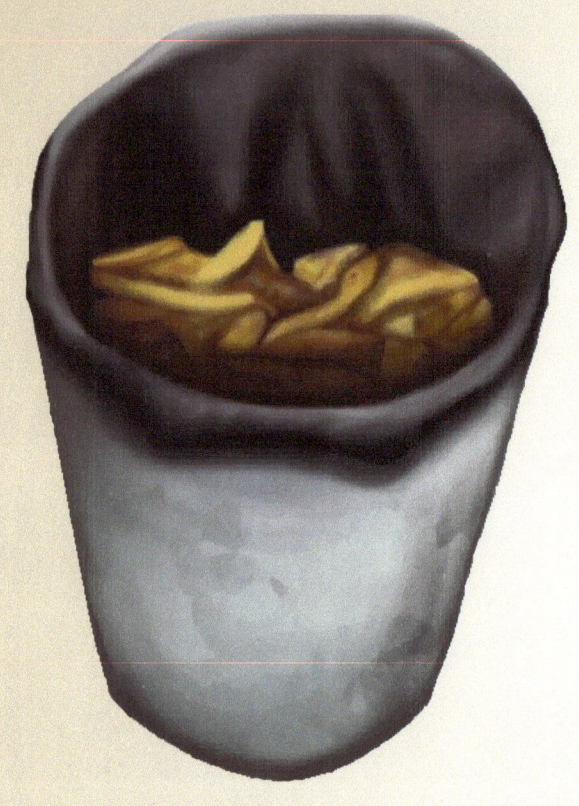

The next day daddy came through the door and said he had bad news. He didn't get paid. He said they were holding a week of pay on him because he just started this new job. He said he drove home on gas fumes. I didn't know what that meant at the time but I soon figured that one out. My mom just looked at him. She didn't say a word. She went into the kitchen, got in the trash and pulled out the skins of the potatoes that she peeled last night. She ran them under cold water, dried them off and fried them up.

Everyone got a little something to eat that night. She looked at daddy and said, we will get through this. Remember I just made somethin' out of less than nothin'.

We got up bright and early the next day and we went to my grandfather and nanny's house. My dad put his guns behind the seat of the truck. As we pulled into my grandfather and nanny's house all the kids got off of the back of the pickup truck and ran to the backyard to play. I stayed back and hung around my dad. Remember, I like to listen and learn about everything, even when I wasn't supposed to. You would probably say I was a nosey kid, but that is how I learned about what was going on. My dad was talking to my grandfather and showing him his guns.

19

My grandfather reached into his pocket, pulled some money out, and gave it to my dad and my dad gave my grandfather his guns. My grandfather said, "they'll be here when you want them back". My father always said guns were like having money in the bank. I guess that's why my grandfather gave him money for them. When we left my grandparents home we went straight to the gas station and filled up the truck, and then went to the grocery store. We all stayed on the truck while my mom and dad went in to get groceries. We had a good dinner that night.

As I became an adult and looked back at my own life, I know that teachers should not talk about children that way. I know that no adult should talk about children that way. I also know that I am somethin' and I am important. All children are somethin'. I do think life has a funny way of molding you into the person that you are today. All that bad stuff about hearing you are nothin' and not having food to eat led me to do the things I do today.

I did become a teacher, just like Mrs. Days said. Also, an administrator, and a supervisor who gets to work with teachers. One of my most important jobs though is to make sure students have a great day. I always give hugs and try my best to make each student smile when I see them.

I grow a big garden every year and I can produce for my family. I give canned food to C-Cap and Salvation Army because a long time ago, they gave to me. I grow a lot of potatoes and tomatoes every year! I can over 100 quarts of each and I give away a lot. I figured if I could give others who don't have food like I didn't have when I was growing up, they would have somethin' to make out of nothin' too. A 10 lb bag of potatoes would keep them from going hungry and they would never feel like they were nothin'.

It's funny how a couple of words from so many years ago sticks with you. -Somethin' out of nothin' I hope you believe that you are something and I hope you remember that people are people and no one is any better or any worse than the next. We all have to help one another. Someone once told me you can't ever put scrambled eggs back together. I am almost glad that those teachers were talking about me because I can make a beautiful omelet out of scrambled eggs today.

So, when you think you are nothin' - make somethin' out of nothin'.

To Students,

Always believe you are something no matter where you come from. Know that your parents are doing better than their parents, and you will do better than your parents financially.

- Believe in yourself.
- Believe in others.
- Give when you can and even when you can't.
- Try not to judge others, and most of all be YOU!
- Be YOU!
- Be different!
- Stand out!

YOU are the gift to the world. YOU are going to have a big impact on this world. Take a risk and invent something that the world needs. Do something different! It is YOU that will make a difference. It is you that will see the past in order to make positive change for the future. It is YOU who we need to believe in. Most importantly to you, is to be your best advocate. When you don't understand something, stop them and ask again. Make sure you ask questions no matter how many times you need to ask. Persevere and push forward. Work hard–it always pays off. Don't give up! You can do this!

I believe in YOU!

To Teachers,

Our most vulnerable students are those who live in poverty. Those who have generations before them that lived in poverty. Sometimes poverty is plain as day and sometimes it is hidden. The one thing you can do for impoverished students is to first build a relationship that is sincere and authentic. Show them you are listening. When they don't have a pencil, have pencils ready for all, when you know they didn't get breakfast, have snacks available but more importantly than anything else is believe in that child and have high expectations for them. Do not give up on them and make sure they know you believe in them. Give them opportunities to shine! Help them open doors that don't exist. Always put yourself in the shoes of the student. And, never, ever judge a student or speak badly about students.

The stress on students who live in poverty can have a negative impact on them and prevent them from succeeding in school. When a student comes to school and thinks about what they're going to have or not have to eat when he/she goes home they have a real hard time concentrating on school. Try to remember that when they are behind with instruction, it's not because they don't care, it's because they can't care. It's not because they are lazy. It's not because they are dumb. It's because they are trying to figure out life and survive in the world that you may not know exists. So, try to remember that when they are not the first one to answer a question and they look like they are not paying attention. Try to remember that you may be their only saving grace. So, most importantly know your students and let them know you care. Never give up on students. Never speak inappropriately about any student and most of all give it your all every day. Seek to teach instead of reprimand! You can do this!

I believe in YOU!

To Parents

Talk to your child. Let them know you care. If you are living in poverty the best thing you can do is read to your child. Show them how important education is. Take them to the library. Take them to art museums, nature walks, and community events. Children living in poverty don't have an extensive vocabulary due to the number of books in the house. This can be prevented. The public library is FREE. Start when your children are young.

My mom used to drop me off at the public library every Friday night. I would get to stay there for hours. I would read, I would watch how others interacted. I would watch families come in and check out books. This is one of my happiest childhood memories.

Check in with your child. If you can't help them with school work, talk to their teacher. If they can't help you, talk to the principal. You are your child's biggest advocate. If you need financial support, reach out to the school and they can share resources that can help. Most of all never give up and keep working hard. You can do this.

I believe in YOU!

Poverty and Our Children

We are seeing generational poverty more so than ever today. One in six children in America live in poverty. Poverty goes across all races. Poor children are more likely to drop out of school, become unemployed, live on government subsidy, experience economic hardship, and be involved in the criminal justice system.

Our best fight against poverty is education.

Start with something easy!

    If you are ever in a situation when you are trying to make ends meet, start to think about the future and begin to plan ahead. When you are poor, you live day to day. It is hard to see the future because you are always worried about today. One way to look toward the future is to begin thinking about growing a garden. The control that you have over not going hungry and feeding your children is no doubt very hard, but growing your own food is one of the most rewarding things you will ever do, and it puts you in control of your future. The harder you work the more produce you reap. This process allows you to begin to change your mindset and look toward the future instead of day by day. You can do this. You can grow vegetables no matter where you live!

How to grow potatoes no matter where you live!

   Potatoes can grow most anywhere. A planter, a raised bed, a bucket, an old tire, or a garden. Sometimes the potatoes you bring home from the store begin to get eyes on them and you can cut the eyes off and peel them and fry them up but you can also save a few and put them in a paper bag in a dark place in the fall and winter months and keep them until spring.

A Little About Growing Potatoes!

I live in the eastern panhandle of West Virginia so I plant my potatoes after St. Patrick's Day in the spring of the year. I rarely buy planting potatoes. Every year I put a bushel or so back for next year's crop. I plant them in the garden rather than the raised beds because it yields more. If you don't have space, find a bucket, put some holes in the bottom, add some dirt or topsoil about half way full then add the potatoes. You will want to take the potato that has eyes on it (the little plants that grow from the potato) cut the potato up so it has about three eyes on each piece of the potato. (An old tire can be used by following the same steps but when the season is over, pick up the tire and the potatoes will roll right out.) Let the potatoes set out for a few days after cutting into pieces with the eyes on them before you plant. Then put two or three pieces in the bucket then fill to the top with more soil. Keep it watered and in the sunlight. In about twelve to sixteen days, your potatoes begin to germinate. Green plants start to pop and before you know it you have a large, thick green plant. Potato plants are beautiful. After the plant grows you will begin to see white flowers. I let my plants die off completely, then I harvest. To harvest potatoes from the bucket, just tip the bucket over and begin to sift through the soil and find your "gold!" You can expect about fifty pounds of potatoes from 2 lbs of seed potatoes.

How to fry potatoes!

Any skillet will do, cast iron is one of my favorites! You have the option of peeling the potatoes or leaving the skins on. Slice your potatoes up thin. Add lard or oil to you skillet, begin on medium heat. Let potatoes brown for 3-4 minutes and then flip so that both sides are golden brown. You can add onions and fry them when you are frying your potatoes. Add salt and pepper to taste and enjoy! Potatoes are a wonderful inexpensive food that goes a long way. So many other ways to make potatoes and it can stand alone as a meal! Don't ever go hungry with just a few potatoes.

About The Author

Dr. Sharon F. Shrum currently lives in West Virginia. She writes children's books and has worked in public education for over 25 years. Her life has been dedicated to helping children not only academically but socially and emotionally as well. She has a passion for improving education and life's outcomes for systemically marginalized children, which is also the driving force for her life and career.

The book, Somethin' Out of Nothin' is her debut novel. She has several other literature projects still in the works. Sharon believes one of the biggest things that breaks poverty is education. Many times, quitting school goes hand in hand with poverty. A person's likelihood of not completing high school when in poverty is higher than those not living in poverty. Once a student has dropped out of school, the cycle of poverty can continue to grow. Sharon believes that education is key to breaking generational poverty.

Sharon owns CI&A, LLC (Curriculum, Instruction, & Assessment, LLC) since 2006, and has provided professional learning to teachers in the District of Columbia, Virginia, and West Virginia. Her education has led her to be a leader in the field as well as continue to help change the lives of students. She also teaches courses at local colleges, within her district, and has been on committees to support equity for all children.

Generational poverty can be broken! I am a product of breaking the patterns. I am the first person in my family to go to college. My children are the second generation to break the cycle by being college graduates. When we are three generations out we have a much better success rate of not falling back into poverty. Education is key to breaking generational poverty.

Reach out to **https://ged.com/contact_us/** to get your General Equivalent Diploma.

About the Illustrator

Sandy Woodward is an artist, registered nurse, wife, and mom from Virginia. Her passion for art began at a young age and continued throughout her adult life. She found a new passion in college for the medical field and shifted her focus to obtaining a degree in nursing. However, she continues to enjoy expressing herself through her artwork and has had the opportunity to work on various art projects throughout her community. She loves spending time with her son, Oliver, and husband, Wesley.

In Memory of Emma Jean Dawson

    I dedicate this book to my mom. She modeled for me compassion for others by giving when you have very little to give. She modeled for me strength, grit, and perseverance no matter what life throws your way. Most of all, she modeled for me love, which she showed in her own way. No matter what we didn't have, we always had love, and she showed us how to always make somethin' out of nothin'.

Dedication

To Rob, Desi, Shelbi, and Robbie, thank you for believing in me and encouraging me with your excitement. Always remember you can do anything you put your mind to!

To my sister, Becky Jackson, your excitement about the book was genuine and encouraging every step of the way. You have always made sure I was ok and you have always been there to celebrate my achievements. Your anticipation and always asking me about the book along the way shows me how much you care and believe in me. I love you always.

To administrators and teachers everywhere, build relationships with your students. Know that you are a role model for our students and you have the power to change the trajectory of a child's life. Every child is just one adult away from a success story. Seek to teach before you reprimand. Have high expectations and believe that all students have potential.

To students, believe in yourself. You matter! You are important! You CAN be anything you want!

SOMETHIN' OUT OF NOTHIN'

Text copyright ©2023 Sharon F. Shrum, Illustrations copyright© Sharon F. Shrum.
Original text created by Sharon F. Shrum
First Published in the United States of America
All rights reserved.

No part of this publication may be reproduced, stored in a retrieval system, or transmitted, in any form, or by any means, electrical, mechanical, photocopying, recording or otherwise without prior permission from Sharon F. Shrum.

sharonshrum7@gmail.com for all inquiries.

Website: www.sharonshrum.com

www.ingramcontent.com/pod-product-compliance
Lightning Source LLC
Chambersburg PA
CBHW041436010526
44118CB00002B/90